Survivor's Nuggets:
Walking Through the Stages of Grief to Find Hope

Dawn Cochrane King

Survivor's Nuggets

Survivor's Nuggets:
Walking Through the Stages of Grief to Find Hope

Dawn Cochrane King, Author

Daryln Cochrane, Editor

Dawn Cochrane King
2020

Survivor's Nuggets: Walking Through the Stages of Grief to Find Hope

Copyright © 2020 by Dawn Cochrane King

All rights reserved. This book or any portion thereof may not be reproduced or transmitted in any form or by any means, electronic or mechanically, including photocopying, recording, or by any information storage or retrieval system, without the express written permission of the author except for the use of brief quotations in a book review or scholarly journal. Your support of the author's rights is appreciated. Some names and identifying details have been changed to protect the privacy of individuals. This book is not intended as a substitute for the advice of licensed counselors, therapists, or physicians. The reader should regularly consult a physician in matters relating to his/her health and particularly with respect to any symptoms that may require diagnosis or medical attention.

First Printing: 2020

ISBN 978-1-7354844-0-2

Library of Congress Control Number: 2020920705

Edited by Daryln Cochrane

Cover Art by DeeStyle

Cover Design by Dawn Cochrane King

Published in the United States by Dawn Cochrane King, Nevada

Website: https://www.thejourneylessons.com

Email: authordawnking@gmail.com

Facebook: bit.ly/JourneyCommunity

Instagram: @dawncochraneking

Dedication

I lovingly dedicate this book to "Aunt" Irma Knox for opening the door and guiding me through my bereavement ministry journey.

I also dedicate this book to loved ones whose stories did not reach these pages. My memories of them are forever written on my heart:

Mama Lily   *Nana*
Daddy George   *Tavi*
Aunt Barbara   *Deidre*
Uncle DeDe   *Uncle Keith*
"The Captain"   *Uncle Rico*
Uncle Curtis   *Uncle HC*
Aunt Denyce   *Aunt Josephine*
Uncle Tony   *LaVonne*
Aunt Shirley   *Evelyn S.*
Pjay   *Ann*
Ms. Barbara   *Ms. Peggy*
Evelyn D.   *Aunt Doris*
Dene   *Susie*
Karen "KK"   *Harold*
Frances   *Ms. Treadwell*

Survivor's Nuggets

Table of Contents

Acknowledgements ix
Preface 2
Introduction 3
Facing Fear 5
Grief and Loss 12
The Stages of Grief 15
Finding Value 43
Extra Nuggets 49
Survivor's Nuggets: The Journal 71
Survivor's Nuggets: Write Your Life Story 76
Conclusion 86
References 89
Notes 90

Acknowledgements

I thank God for inspiration, provision, and purpose. Special gratitude abounds for my mother for sweet conversation; my father for his appreciation of nostalgia; my family and friends for experiences and loving memories; my pastors for their teaching and preaching; my daughter for the spirit of joy and hope; and my devoted husband for love, support, and laughter.

I also thank the CEO Wife's Writer's Community for Women and the countless writers who have touched my soul and inspired me to share my stories.

A special thank you goes to my sister for our special connection and for bringing clarity to my words. Working with her as my editor has been pure joy.

Preface

Dear Reader,

The purpose of Survivor's Nuggets is to help you find hope and value in the midst of loss and to write your life story. Finding value in the midst of loss may sound impossible or ridiculous. I promise it isn't. As you read, I hope you'll identify the stages of grief you find yourself in and the wisdom to seek help when you feel "stuck" in any particular stage. By sharing my stories, I intend to help you discover hope after loss.

I had a glorious opportunity to write my aunt's life story. She was a woman who was in control. She was driven and lived according to her own plan. It was no surprise when she shared that she wanted to write her life story—she actually called it her bio. She explained how she didn't want someone else to have to do it after her death. I immediately offered to help. I'd never written an obituary or a eulogy. But my response was without hesitation or remorse. I sincerely wanted and felt I needed to do it. I will share what that experience was like and why I believe more of us should write our life story and assist others in doing the same.

Thank you for turning the pages and going on this journey. I hope you embrace Survivor's Nuggets to make your journey through loss more hopeful.

Sincerely,

Dawn Cochrane King

Introduction

The phone rings, and you hear words you will never forget. Your life is forever changed, and your instinct is to say no in disbelief. Your loved one has died. Whether a sudden death following an accident or the end of life after a long battle with cancer, the loss is deeply felt. You are grieving. My hope and prayer are that you'll better understand the grief process after reading this book. I've written *Survivor's Nuggets* to walk you through the stages of grief to find hope and learn the benefits of writing your life story.

Once you find yourself in one or more of the stages of grief, what do you do? Some choose to say, "I'm okay," ignore feelings, move on, or go through the motions of getting back to *normal*. Sadly, this is too often the case. Rushing to get back to normal causes you to miss out on the rewards. These rewards or *nuggets* are found after genuinely acknowledging the stages of grief and ultimately finding value in going through the process.

For years, I feared death. Many who know me as a former bereavement ministry director and hospice volunteer would find that shocking. I rarely talked about it. The fear was at its peak when my daughter was a toddler. Oh, how I prayed that I would live long enough to see her become an independent adult. I said this prayer along with my daily prayers—yes, every single day. I wasn't ill, and I didn't have a dangerous or life-threatening job. My fear was not based on facts, but when you own fear, you create your own facts! I heard the acronym a million times, but it was time

Survivor's Nuggets

to start owning it: FEAR is False Evidence Appearing Real.

Whether fear, anger, guilt, or depression are gripping you due to loss, I wrote this book intending to help you live through it all. I plan to equip you with the tools needed to do the following four essential things:

1. Gain a clear understanding of the stages of grief.
2. Acknowledge the stage(s) of grief you identify with.
3. Discover your *nuggets* of value and hope.
4. Write your life story.

Facing Fear

I was in the middle of a divorce when my daughter was just one-year-old. Although her father remained in her life, I felt alone and afraid of what would happen to her if I died. Despite wanting the divorce, I experienced feeling failure and the strain of having to start a new way of life. What drove me forward was the desire to be a good example for my child. I planned to raise her in a happy household, even if that meant divorcing her father. When the divorce was final a year later, I was relieved yet sad that I had to make that choice. I was sad that the intended *until death do us part* had become a broken promise. I didn't know it then, but I was grieving.

Along with grief, I experienced fear. Fear is so immobilizing. It keeps you stuck where you are for fear of doing something different. The only way to get rid of fear is to face it and take action in spite of it. I can talk that talk now, but not before I learned to walk the walk.

I stated earlier that I rarely talked about my fear of dying. Certainly not to my mother or sister with whom I share so much. I didn't want to burden my family or friends because I believed they needed to know I was okay. I lived so far away from them and did not want them to worry about me. I felt they needed to see that life was great, and I was happy. For the most part, it was, but I could not shake this fear.

Finally, I spoke to a minister after church one day. His response was, "None of us know when we're going to die. Let's say you do die. Do you trust God with your daughter?" The conversation was brief. Yes, I trust God with my child because He gave her to me in the first place. I walked away, feeling like I didn't get what I was looking for, but I asked myself, "What did you expect?" Honestly, what was this person going to say to make this fear magically go away? I figured I had to pray and trust God to help me through it. Praying and trusting God was correct, but there was more. The Bereavement Ministry became a door to so many things I never knew I needed.

I found a new church where I enjoyed the teaching, preaching, and music. Yes! The music was so good. I cried, I laughed, and most of all, I learned. I've attended other churches, but this was the first time I actually learned about a personal relationship with God. Oh, the others were fine. They taught from the bible and aligned with my own beliefs. But I didn't connect with the teachings about this personal relationship. I was growing, learning, and quoting scripture. I was studying the scriptures because they had particular meaning for me. The fear was still lingering, though, and I needed to learn what it meant to have the courage to step outside of my comfort zone. Fear could only exist in my comfort zone. But I didn't know how to step out…yet.

One Sunday, a woman approached me with a kind smile and asked if I would like to attend the next Bereavement Ministry meeting. I politely declined. She found me what seemed like every Sunday for weeks and kept asking. There was that kind smile again. Then, one of the elders approached me with the same question. I was shocked. Why were these people asking me to join the

Bereavement Ministry? They didn't have a clue about me. I softly explained that it would not be a good fit for me because I cry too quickly and would not be able to help. I am a crier. Yes, I cry during Hallmark commercials. I cry each time Angela Bassett as Stella cries about not being able to call her best friend Delilah—played by Whoopi Goldberg—even though I've seen the movie at least 23 times! So imagine the panic that washed over me when asked to attend the Bereavement Ministry meeting.

After I declined the invitation, the elder persisted. He wasn't satisfied with my explanation about being a crier. Instead, he smiled and said, "You'll be perfect then! We need people with compassion and understanding. So we'll see you at the meeting on Saturday?" I nodded and whispered, "Okay." I could have kicked myself all the way to the parking lot. Why didn't I say no? Well, it turned out to be one of the best decisions I ever made.

That very first meeting was fascinating to me. I found myself sharing my most recent experience with death. I spoke about how deeply saddened I was about my grandmother, Mama Lily. I felt guilty about moving so far away from New York and not seeing her as often as I would have if I still lived there. I knew no one in the room, yet several shared intimate experiences of loss they were dealing with. For the first time, I realized how important it was to deal with our own grief in order to help others do the same.

I continued to attend the meetings and closely watched Sister Irma, the director. She attended hospice training and eagerly taught us what she learned. I started reading about the stages of grief, and pretty soon, Sister Irma asked me to create the meeting agenda each week.

I learned what it meant to support a family in their time of mourning. The steps were very methodical, yet each experience was unique. After receiving the call that a church member or relative of a member had died, we went into action. We brought meals to the family's home. If the funeral would be out of town, we sent a card and made phone calls. If held at our church or another local facility, we would gather volunteers to attend the service and serve food at the repast. As you can imagine, there were intricate details involved in each step. Each event brought a sense of normalcy about death. The fear was slowly fading. I promised myself to focus more on living. I knew that my death would be a sad event for those left behind, but sadder if I left goals undone. So I wrote down what I believed was my life's purpose, set goals, and worked at them. I didn't want to accomplish things just to give people something to talk about at my funeral. I wanted to do something that would matter. I wanted to leave my daughter with good memories and the assurance of fulfilling one's purpose. I wrote that my purpose is to help people through some of the most difficult times of their lives. I've found more than one way to work on that purpose; I hope this book is one of them.

Another lesson or nugget learned was this: be quiet and listen. Sure, we learned what to say and, more importantly, what not to say. Knowing when to be silent and listen with an objective ear is soothing for grieving people. That lesson served me well as I continued to help others.

Sister Irma had become Aunt Irma now. We talked often, and she left me in charge more frequently. She groomed me to step in when she was called to direct another ministry of the church. It was an honor for me to accept the invitation to become the Bereavement Ministry Director.

One day, I read my list of sick and shut-in members. Two were in the hospital, and three I had to call. I had get-well cards in my purse and words of encouragement written on my heart. It was especially important to visit Warren because he was extremely ill. I did not know him, but his wife Lena was a fellow church member. She was struggling with the likelihood of losing him. I knew from previous visits that she often refused to eat or go home and rest because she longed to be near him. It may seem like a small thing, but I made it my mission to make sure we visited the cafeteria. The visit, however, went beyond the cafeteria. You see, I knew hospital visits were necessary, and what drove me to go on this particular day was something that tugged at me. That small voice kept saying, "These people only meet you at funerals; they don't know you." I wanted to get to know the families a little better before making arrangements for their loved ones. I wanted them to get to know me and feel comfortable talking to me. So, I visited. I called. And when the inevitable call came, deciding on the repast menu or funeral process was not our first conversation.

Survivor's Nuggets

Because the church is large, it was impossible to know everyone, so these visits were crucial to establishing relationships. When the family decided to take Warren off of life support, Lena called me. I held her hand and prayed with the family while she waited for them to remove his body from ICU. As heartbreaking as that day was, our friendship was more important to Lena than seeing me as a reminder of such a sad day. I often thought seeing me would bring back the sharp memories of her loss, but the opposite happened. She needed to talk without having to explain too much or face judgment. Our experience was another reminder of the need to quietly listen to someone grieving. Lena and I had no history. I didn't know anything about her marriage outside of her experiences in the hospital. I had no opinions and could be the ear she needed. It was during that friendship that I asked her to join the ministry. With a very strong, "No way!" I was still hopeful that she'd join. We'll return to Lena's story later.

As I continued to serve people who were grieving, I began to fear death less and less. I continued to focus on living and not dying. When the fear found its way into my thoughts, I countered with positive thinking. It was during this time that I began talking more often to my grandmother, Nana. She provided the added wisdom about the bible I needed at that time. I'd been attending church regularly for some years at that point in my life. I was confident about talking about scripture and enjoyed conversations with her. Nana shared what she knew in her heart with warm words and conviction. She said we must use all the time God gives us, and that stuck with me. I began to tell myself, "How can I insult God by being afraid to die?" I will forever be grateful for that nugget. I want to live a very long life, but I'm no longer afraid to leave this earth for my heavenly adventure. I learned that being afraid of dying kept me from fully embracing living. I had to finally say and believe that living a full life of 40 years was more precious than living for 90 years and never fulfilling my purpose. We don't have control over how long we live, but we do have control over how we live. If you're living with fear, I pray my story gives you the courage to live with hope.

Grief and Loss

We've all experienced grief and loss. No matter how many times we lose a loved one, each event brings a unique experience.

Serving people during extremely challenging times allowed me to share such unique experiences. For years, I visited hospitals, hospice rooms, and homes. I called the bereaved, took food to families after a loved one's death, sent cards, made phone calls, attended funerals, and coordinated repasts. I was there to serve, to encourage, to listen, and to provide a little company. Serving during such somber times was, in fact, a privilege. I considered it a privilege because I was fulfilling my purpose. I believe my purpose in life is to help others through the most challenging times of their lives.

Throughout the book, I share true stories of who I've lost and what I gained in the process. I also share stories of helping others walk through grief and share what I learned from their experiences. In some cases, it was years before I realized the purpose or value of a particular experience. Time is a beautiful thing. When we use our time to learn and grow, it is incumbent upon us to pass it on. I believe the purpose of loss is to teach the grieving person lessons they can teach others. Maya Angelou said it best, "When you learn, teach" (Winfrey, O., 2011).

As I shared earlier, I kept my fear of dying a secret. Once no longer afraid to confront my fear, I was able to handle stressful situations and guided others to do the same. Truly understanding loss is at the heart of this book's purpose: to help you move from pain to peace by finding nuggets of value after loss. The book ends with a bonus nugget: a guide to writing your life story.

The Stages of Grief

As previously stated, the stages of grief are the same for all losses, yet the process is unique for each person. As the bereavement ministry director, I conducted bi-weekly training sessions. At the heart of each training was a discussion about the stages of grief. Much has been said, debated, and written about the stages of grief. Many people believe they have a clear understanding of these stages, even if they haven't studied or read about them. Experience teaches us a lot, but actual grief training is so valuable.

I became more effective and sensitive about serving people who were grieving as a result of specific training. This training made me reflect on my own life and the end of life as well. My reason for sharing what I've learned and taught about grief is to better equip you, my reader, for your own grief experiences. I am not a licensed therapist or counselor. My recommendations are based on over 20 years of experience as a bereavement director and a registered hospice volunteer. Experience taught me a lot of life lessons I feel compelled to share with you.

I align each of the following true stories with a stage of grief. The legendary Elisabeth Kübler Ross, the author of *On Death and Dying*, introduced the five stages of death. The book focused on what the dying may teach others about living. Years later, Kübler Ross and David Kessler co-authored *On Grief and Grieving*. In this book, the authors focus on the same stages from the viewpoint of people who are grieving. The stages are:

Survivor's Nuggets

1. Denial/Shock
2. Anger
3. Bargaining
4. Depression
5. Acceptance

The stages of grief do not have to be experienced in this order. Still, it is common for people to experience denial or shock initially. Likewise, acceptance is typically experienced as the final stage. If a grieving person returns to one of the other stages after acceptance, it may be due to an unresolved issue or circumstance. Years later, other writers and scholars added additional stages to the list, such as guilt, shame, and reconstruction.

Except for the stage of acceptance, none of the stages are pleasant. No one wants to be in shock or denial. No one desires to be angry. No one seeks to bargain as the result of a death or loss. And no one would choose to be depressed. Regardless of the obvious negative connotations, each stage provides value to the grieving person.

Denial/Shock

Let's examine the initial stage of denial or shock. Have you or someone you know ever been in such extreme physical pain that you fainted? I have. I was in the kitchen area of my college dormitory. My boyfriend, at the time, was visiting as I prepared to make French fries. A large pot filled with bubbling, hot oil was on the burner in front of me. Because I didn't realize it was a bit off-kilter, when I turned to talk to him, the pot went flying off the stovetop. My boyfriend kicked the pot away from us, but not before I felt extreme pain crashing through my left leg. I screamed and passed out. I woke up minutes later in the shower, where several girls who lived on my dorm floor gathered around me. Someone had removed my jeans, and cold water was streaming frantically everywhere. I later learned that oil burns each layer of skin and tissue. Man, how that made the pain linger! My body knew to go into shock to protect me from unbearable pain and fear. Isn't it amazing how our bodies know how to respond when presented with trauma? When we hear bad news, we may react emotionally, mentally, and even physically. Just as my body protected me after being burned, the mind goes into shock when presented with terrible, life-altering news.

Years after the leg-burning incident, I was at work when I received a call from my sister.

"Mama Lily died," she said in a somber voice.

I immediately responded with, "Don't joke like that!" Of course, she would never joke about our grandmother dying, and she certainly wasn't kidding then. I went into immediate denial, which allowed my body and mind to process the news. Denial is like an automatic reflex and is protective. Denial and shock protect us the way fainting protected me from the physical trauma.

Despite the protective benefit of denial and shock, remaining in this stage too long may keep a person from moving toward the final stage of acceptance. In fact, some people choose to continue to live with the protection of denial. Of course, they know the person has died, yet they remain in denial to avoid working through the grief. How many times have you said, *I'm fine* when falling apart inside? Have you ever heard a friend say *I'm okay* even though you know they are not? Admitting that you are not okay would mean facing what's wrong. It is easy to recognize a person in denial when their words and actions contradict one another. When a person says the right things and appears to be functioning well, their denial may go unnoticed. We have to make an effort to check on people who seem to have it all together. They often mask their pain or need for help but should be encouraged to do just the opposite. If this sounds like you, please reach out to someone.

Some people are so accustomed to hiding emotions that any expression of pain causes them to wonder if they're okay. The most common question a grieving person has asked me is, "Is this normal?" While the stages of grief are common, how you experience them is unique. How you feel or react may not seem normal, but it's okay to question your reactions. Questioning may cause you to analyze yourself. Honest self-analysis is a healthy way to move away from the stage of denial/shock. Face what causes you pain and acknowledge your feelings. Doing so will make it easier to express yourself and leave the stage of denial.

My friend Shay's experience with denial and self-reflection is interesting. She is a minister and someone I often confided in. While working in the ministry together, we talked more often than we do now. She always ended our telephone conversations with prayer—I mean specific prayers that let me know she heard my concerns. Good leaders are good listeners, too.

Shay is the one who always appears focused and is quick to find humor in life's events. Our telephone calls often begin with, "Okay, praise report." One of us shares good news while the other rejoices in genuine happiness. Ultimately Shay laughs and says, "Happy, happy, joy, joy"—a title she's given to her praise dance when celebrating. "Love you, bye," is how we end the quick but meaningful chat. She's the perfect example of the positive attitude that can come from one with great faith. Imagine my surprise when she called me for advice.

The day she called to tell me she didn't cry when her brother died brought a new dynamic to our friendship. This call came quite a while after he passed away.

"Am I okay?" she asked.

Wow. I mentally said a quick prayer. *Lord, please give me the words she needs to hear.*

"Did you grieve for him?"

"Yes. I grieved but not with tears. My brother had been through a lot. I knew he was saved when he died, so I was happy for his soul," she answered in a very matter-of-fact tone. Because I know her, I knew she wasn't being cold or uncaring. She was being sincere.

"Seriously, do you think I'm okay?" I took my time to explain that not everyone grieves the same way. I acknowledged that she has a particular way of not worrying. She genuinely trusts the Lord for everything. I didn't use the word *denial*, but I certainly thought about it. I didn't want to discount her positive outlook. I didn't want to discourage her from believing in hope. Some may misunderstand her disposition, but I believe she was her authentic self. Even when she was admitted to the hospital, and the doctors were a bit grim about her diagnosis, she told me she considered her hospital stay a vacation and went to sleep.

"I can't let these people worry me. I'm already healed. Anyway, to die is gain; I'll be in heaven." Thankfully, she did recover. Shay was released from the hospital, but I never forgot her response to her illness.

As much as I understood her statements and how they align with the bible, I also believed she might be in denial about her brother. Because she is such a positive person, displaying joy and a lack of worry may seem necessary. As I explained earlier, expressing one thing when you feel another is a form of denial. The stage of denial is one we cannot gloss over. We should not dismiss it once the initial shock of a loss is felt. Denial can linger as I believe it did for Shay.

    I reminded her that others might react as she did, but perhaps not initially. They may eventually say similar words about their loved one being in heaven or a better place. However, in my experience, such words comfort people later. That comfort comes after the tears, anger, regret, and sorrow. Shay skipped these steps but never acknowledged it until she questioned if she was okay. She never thought of her reactions as odd. Now, after not crying while mourning his death, she wondered if she was okay. The self-analysis is what caused her to question if her response was acceptable. I believed that was a good sign. It was a sign that Shay was moving away from the protection of denial. We cannot hide under the protective cover of denial forever because it causes us to hide emotions. Shay was ready to express those emotions or at least consider why she hadn't cried. I told her not to be surprised if something unexpected brought her to tears for her brother; a song, a movie, a favorite meal, or a familiar fragrance. All the little things recognized by our five senses often awaken memories and spark tears. In the meantime, I assured her that she was alright.

    Nugget: Always remember that people we look to for guidance have their fragile moments as well. They grieve as we all do, and we need to check on them. They are strong yet human. We're here to strengthen, encourage, and love them, too. Shay is a staple on the altar of our church. Many turn to her for prayer and advice, and she was asking me for help. The leaders in your life may be pillars of strength, but they also need to be strengthened and assured. Maybe that's you. As a leader at home, work, church, or other organization, are you expected to be the strong one? Do you put that burden on yourself when you're the one grieving? If you're expected to be strong, you may find yourself saying, "I'm okay," even when you're not. This keeps you from grieving and is an often unnoticed form of denial. I encourage you to share your feelings. Verbalizing what she was feeling about herself allowed Shay to leave the stage of denial. Self-reflection may help you do the same.

Anger

Anger is a stage of grief that often results in negative expressions. Crying, feeling resentment and extreme disappointment are natural feelings of anger. When expressed in negative or unhealthy ways, the grieving person engages in verbal outbursts, strikes or destroys objects, or argues. There is nothing wrong with being angry. You have good reason to be. How you express your anger and respond to it will determine how you experience this stage.

As I stated, anger is a normal emotion. It's even okay to be angry at the person who died. The hardest part will be letting go of the anger. Although you may not want to feel angry, trying to stop the anger can be overwhelming. When anger builds up, you might have the urge to drink it away, overeat, take it out on someone who is not at fault, become violent, or start arguments. You might feel relieved after doing any of the above, but that kind of relief is usually temporary.

Healthy ways to release anger include screaming into a pillow, hitting a punching bag, exercising, singing loudly, or playing an instrument. None of the above magically makes anger disappear. These activities allow you to direct your rage to something productive or harmless. In time, the rage will lessen. You are still grieving, but hopefully, you are no longer on the verge of acting irrationally.

Writing in a journal or meditating may be helpful when you need to calm down; however, some may oppose meditation. In fact, a very angry person might become even angrier if someone suggests they meditate. Choose healthy ways to make yourself feel better.

Let's return to the story about my friend, Lena. She's the one who called to tell me they were removing her husband, Warren, from life support. He died in the hospital just minutes before I arrived. She experienced deep sadness and loneliness. Eventually, she created new routines without Warren. One of the most critical things Lena did was admit she was angry.

Warren was part of her everyday routine, habits, and life; she couldn't adjust to the possibility of life without him. I met Lena for the first time at the hospital, but, as I stated earlier, she was a familiar face at church. We clicked like a key in a lock as soon as I stepped into the quiet room.

Survivor's Nuggets

After the initial small talk and introductions, she looked at her husband. His soft hair blended nicely with the crisp white pillow beneath his head. He was non-responsive. Lena was a combination of a wife trying to get her husband up for work and a little girl waiting for Daddy to get home. Pulling out my bible to share a scripture or to pray was, at that moment, removed from my agenda. I discerned that she needed her physical needs met before she could digest spiritual food. After intently listening to Lena describe Warren's medical condition and experiences over the last few weeks, I urged her to walk with me to the cafeteria. As she picked at her food, I asked her to eat a little something every two to three hours to keep herself well. I could see that eating an entire meal at once would be a real chore. As I left the hospital, I prayed for Warren and Lena. Before I reached my car, I also sent up prayers of encouragement for every patient and their loved ones. And as always, I thanked God for using me and allowing me to walk in and out of a hospital one more time.

I kept in touch with Lena and often prayed with her during the following weeks. One night after dinner, my phone rang, "They're taking him off life support tonight." Lena spoke in a soft, staccato-like voice. I grabbed my jacket and purse and headed toward the garage. I let Lena know I was on my way before she had a chance to ask me if I would come. Warren died just moments before I reached his room. Lena's small frame sunk into my arms. I held her quietly. She was surrounded by her sisters, her son, and her niece. I prayed for strength and peace as we waited for someone to remove her precious Warren's body.

With time, Lena grew stronger. She eventually accepted my invitation to join the bereavement ministry. Being busy and helping others gave her a new purpose and something to look forward to. Her voice was still a whisper when she said, Warren, but she cried a little less often. I witnessed her ability to laugh at times when she talked about him. A pivotal moment happened the day she admitted she was angry. I couldn't leave it at that. I asked her what she would like to do about it.

"About what?" she asked with a look of surprise and curiosity on her face.

"What do you want to do about your anger?" That question started a lengthy conversation. Ultimately, Lena admitted that she needed to let go of the anger. She said she realized she was angry at Warren for leaving her. On the surface, her words may sound odd or even selfish, but I applaud her honesty. Her anger was not full of rage. She quietly made statements like, "I can't believe he left me" or "Now I have to do this by myself." Initially, I simply listened. In time, I asked if she was angry. She started to answer but then stopped. I sat quietly with her. She seemed to be thinking. I'll never forget the look on her face when I asked her what she wanted to do about her anger. It was a turning point in her grief journey. For years following Warren's death, Lena continued to enjoy working in the ministry.

Survivor's Nuggets

Like so many *survivor's nuggets*, the nugget of wisdom in Lena's story can only be found after triumphing over tragedy. After being tormented with grief, sadness, anger, and what feels like a loss of control, you can find purpose. Lena was able to touch the lives of other people who lost loved ones. She was excited to join a small group we created to serve widows. She found joy in gathering with them. Her test became her testimony. Again, no one longs to be angry about death, but I hope you can see what life can become during and after the grieving process. When you feel as if you have no purpose and depression or anger is about to win the fight, stand up and fight a little longer. It is no cliché; joy can and will come in the morning.

Bargaining

The stage of grief, known as bargaining, is very interesting. I say it's interesting because it may seem like a completely ludicrous thing when on the outside looking in. In the bargaining stage, a person grieving a painful loss begins to make deals psychologically. They find themselves saying things like *I promise to be a better parent for the rest of my life if I could wake up from this nightmare and hold my child again.* What's important here is that the person has moved from denial or shock to trying to do something to make it all go away. Bargaining is unrealistic thinking. However, it does imply that the person understands the loss is real and is no longer in denial or shock. Hopefully, reaching this stage means moving a bit closer to acceptance.

While a terminally ill patient suffers, bargaining seems quite natural. Bargaining with God to save someone's life may sound like, "God, I promise to be a better sister if you just let my brother live." Don't get me wrong; I fervently believe in prayer. However, prayers are not contingent upon a person striking a deal or bargaining with God. He never promised that if we do something for Him, he would answer our prayers exactly the way we want Him to. God does promise never to leave us during our struggles.

While grieving, if you find yourself saying "if only… or what if…," you're most likely in the bargaining stage. Although guilt has not been named a stage of grief, it is often associated with bargaining or other stages. Bargaining is a way to take a break from grief or guilt while fantasizing about how life would be if only_ _ _ _ _. During times like these, I suggest you write your feelings down. As stated earlier, writing in a journal at various times throughout the grieving process is cathartic. Journaling helps you to release emotions you may not have shared with anyone. Reading your journal weeks, months, or even years after writing in them allows you to see how far you've come.

The process of writing about our journey through grief allows us actually to do something. When we lose someone, we often feel so helpless. We are not in control and cannot *fix* the situation. But when we express authentic thoughts on paper, we often feel a sense of release and relief. We can't hold onto feelings of guilt, anger, depression, or other emotions associated with the grief stages. Holding on to any of them would only make us immobile, lack the motivation to do anything, and make us unpleasant to be around.

I had an *if only* experience with my friend Avery. I miss hearing him say, "Hey, Sis." We had a friendship that started when he was in the hospital. He was admitted again, and again, I was visiting. These visits to the sick and recuperating had become part of my routine. I'm there with the patients to encourage and listen, share a kind word, and then listen some more. It's a bonus when a patient becomes a friend.

Avery had intense pain and was afraid. Countless times my phone would ring. I'd answer only to hear his sounds of despair and pain. He was usually ready to sleep just before we hung up.

He had a distinctive conservative flair for styling his hair, setting a table, decorating a room, and choosing the perfect clothing and shoes to look dapper. His walk was as if he'd just stepped off the runway, heading to the cover of GQ. He exuded style and confidence.

It was hard to imagine that picture of confidence was the same person crying on the phone because his painkillers weren't doing a thing for him. So I shared scriptures until he started quoting them for himself. My sharing was just a reminder. Avery knew all about the scriptures he grew up reading. He often spoke lovingly of his parents, sister, and nieces. Avery and his sister shared tender childhood memories and a thriving relationship as adults. He smiled as he talked about how they both knew every word of dialogue and lyrics in the movie *The Wiz* because they watched it so many times together. When visiting his home, he popped the movie into his VCR. As he braided my daughter's hair, his booming voice vibrated through the air during each song. I closed my eyes and let his deep, rich voice bring me back to the day I enjoyed *The Wiz* on Broadway.

Here he was in the hospital again. He was freezing just as he described on the phone the day before. I quietly entered his room with an electric blanket and a smile.

"Thanks, Sis, I really appreciate this." Avery affectionately called me "Sis," although not related. We were, however, members of the same church family.

"Sure," I answered, taking the soft navy blue blanket out of the package. "How are you today?"

"I'm scared." He started crying. I told him that God didn't give him a spirit of fear, and then I prayed that God would give him the strength and courage to go through whatever lies ahead—no matter what. Our eyes locked when I said, "No matter what," and he slowly nodded. An unspoken understanding hung in the air as I caught myself holding my breath. He never exactly told me his diagnosis, but his symptoms were pretty severe and progressively worsening. I always prayed for comfort, strength, and peace. I continued to call and visit him regularly and enjoyed our visits as much as he seemed to enjoy them.

Months later, my mother decided to join me during another visit to the hospital. On this day, Avery smiled and said he was happy. He went on to say he was very grateful to God for love, family, and friends—something he often spoke of before this visit. The stages of grief culminate with acceptance. Perhaps he grieved for himself long enough. He seemed content with life and ready to accept what may come. Suddenly, both his cell phone and the hospital room phone rang; a reminder of the many people who cared about him. We hugged him and walked out. The tapping of our heels on the shiny floors drowned out the silence. It was the solemn silence found in hospital hallways as we started the long walk toward the elevator.

During a call a few weeks later, Avery sounded especially energetic.

"Hey, Sis! How are you? Yes, I have a few people visiting." I could hear voices, and he was happily laughing when he picked up the phone.

"Well, enjoy your visit, Brother. I can talk to you later." Later never came. I left a voicemail message on his cell phone the next day. Then he left a voice message for me; our last game of phone tag.

On December 17, 2004, late evening: my phone rings. "Hey, girl," the voice of my sweet friend, Lonna, was on the other end. For years, she and I shared stories of how Avery could make us both laugh and how well he cooked.

"I just got a call. They said Avery passed?" Lonna said, seeking confirmation. "Have you heard anything?"

"No," I said in disbelief. I don't care how many times we get this call; somehow, we go into denial.

"I just spoke to him last week," I said, as if that meant he had to be okay. "Don't start worrying. Let me call his sister, and I'll call you back." After confirming that Avery was truly gone, I called her back. "It's true, girl."

Lonna and I cried together on the phone. Her first words were of regret. "I feel so bad. I didn't go see him the last time he was in the hospital. I can't believe it."

I had regrets to deal with, too. My last words to Avery were recorded on voice mail. Why didn't I call one more time? Now it's too late. I thought about this until the day of his memorial service. Do you see how I started to bargain? If only I had called him one more time. Well, that would not have changed the outcome. Yet it's natural for us to think there must be something we could have done differently. On that day, I felt like I should have assured him that I was thinking about him.

Survivor's Nuggets

On the day of his memorial service, it hit me. It was then that I remembered the email. I have received several email messages and cards from Avery over the years, but one in particular was printed and saved. It was folded in half and tucked into my study bible. The date and time read: 11/27/03, 6:17:52 PM Pacific Standard Time, and the subject read, "It's your brother." The message erased my regret and guilt. That email wrapped me in a hug. Here's what he wrote:

Hey Sis,

Thank you for being part of my Thanksgiving; it meant the world to me. Thanksgiving is a time to be with friends, family, and those that love you. You mean the world to me, and I am so grateful God brought you into my life.

"Such is friendship that through it we love places and seasons; for as bright bodies emit rays to a distance, and flowers drop their sweet leaves on the ground around them, so friends impart favor even to the places where they dwell. With friends, even poverty is pleasant. Words cannot express the joy which a friend imparts; they only can know who have experienced. A friend is dearer than the light of heaven, for it would be better for us that the sun were exhausted than that we should be without friends."
        –Saint John Chrysostom

Thanks for being my friend.

Much love, your brother,
Avery

Saying goodbye to Avery was a reminder to be kind to myself. Through the grief process, I urge you to be kind to yourself. Acknowledge each of the stages: denial and shock, anger, bargaining, depression, and acceptance. Tell yourself it's okay to feel anger, guilt, regret, or shame during each of these stages. Remember to do frequent self-checks. Ask yourself if you've been in a particular stage too long. Only you—or a counselor or therapist, if necessary—can determine what is too long for you.

None of the stages should hinder you from welcoming acceptance. The stage of acceptance does not mean you are now happy with the loss. Nor does acceptance mean you are *over it*—there is no such thing. Acceptance means that you acknowledge that you cannot change it and are ready to come to terms with it. Those you lost would want you to continue to live and not merely exist. Your loved one wants you to live with hope in spite of grief. Allow yourself to experience each stage in a healthy way. Be kind to yourself, and embrace acceptance. I believe you will ultimately find value in the process.

Avery's message allowed him to express his gratitude for our friendship. He wrote it one year before he died. He was well-loved, so I like to think that he found peace in sharing similar words of gratitude with others. His message gives me closure. No matter what emotion I feel when remembering him or which stage of grief I relate to at any given moment, I know our friendship had purpose. I did not readily recognize this until he was gone. I no longer regret not calling one more time. The nugget I found was the gratitude that replaced regret.

Depression

Depression is a stage of grief that often results in isolation or seclusion. You may welcome being alone and the peace of solitude to be sad, cry, and think. I encourage you to embrace those quiet times. Just as important as finding solitude is the need for you to be aware of your responses. Be careful about saying no to all invitations to spend time with others. If you're going out of your way to avoid people, you may need to ask for help. The state of feeling deeply sad is normal. However, if you find that you're isolating yourself for long periods of time, it may be time to seek professional help. I realize a long period of time is relative. What is long to one person may not be long for you. Being honest with yourself is crucial. Are you avoiding people even if it means no longer engaging in your favorite activities? If your answer is *yes*, I can't stress enough how important it is to get help. Consider talking to a friend or a counselor.

It is also imperative to remember that your friends and family have good intentions. They might try to *fix* the situation. This is a perfect opportunity for you to reminisce about your loved one. Help them to see that you're expressing a natural reaction to death. These conversations create an informal support network. Those who are depressed and welcome interaction with others are on their way to getting through the loss. Sadly, the opposite was true for my friend Devra. Her story lacks the happy ending of finding hope. I'm sharing it with you because it is filled with nuggets nonetheless.

Devra was a cheerful woman in her fifties. We often saw each other at church. One day, Devra asked me to help her mother, Janine, to sell her home. I was a real estate agent at the time and welcomed the referral. What began as a professional relationship quickly turned to friendship. After I gave her tips to stage her home for potential buyers, Janine shared her diagnosis.

"I have cancer, and I don't want to spend the rest of my life taking care of this house," Janine explained with a giggle. She was so cute, and her eyes twinkled each time she smiled.

"In today's market, your home will sell quickly," I assured her.

During our phone calls and visits about the house, Janine often talked about Devra. She was concerned about her and was so glad we were friends. I was friendly with Devra, but we weren't exactly friends. I barely knew her. Janine shared how difficult Devra's life had been and that she was now back on track. Janine was so proud that Devra was living in her own apartment and going to church again. Her face beamed as she explained that her daughter had been sober for so long. Even though no one else was in the house, Janine whispered that she watched her daughter struggle with drugs for years.

My daughter and I continued to visit Janine while her home was in escrow and after it sold. At eight-years-old, my daughter met Janine, and they bonded immediately. Janine had a lovely way of making the simplest things seem so special. She would cut a peach in slices before serving it to us. As she set the plate and forks on the table, Janine would smile and say, "Now we will eat like ladies." My daughter loved our visits, and so did I.

Sadly, Janine's condition became worse, and the doctors could do nothing more about the spreading cancer.

Our last visit was in Janine's hospice room, where she asked me to sign a couple of documents as a witness. Janine also asked me to look after Devra and said, "I know you know what I mean, right?" She posed that last question with her twinkling smile on her face. She died five days later.

Devra continued to do well until her mother died. She kept telling me she didn't know what she was going to do. She needed her mother and couldn't imagine life without her. I assured Devra that her mother would want her to continue to live her life and take good care of herself. I reminded Devra of how proud her mother was of her. As I spoke, I knew my words were falling on deaf ears. Devra had given up. The depression had gotten to the point that she no longer saw a reason to go on. She'd lost the ultimate hope: to live in spite of the pain. I did what I could. I called a family member to express my concern, and I prayed for her.

The day of Janine's funeral arrived. She looked so pretty, as if smiling while taking a peaceful nap. Devra approached me to give me a hug, and there it was; the smell of alcohol. My heart sank.

Weeks before she died, Janine promised a few trinkets from her curio cabinet to my daughter. Devra never denied that, but she hesitated to set a date for me to visit and retrieve them. When she stopped answering the phone, I went to see her out of concern. She opened the door with a crooked smile, and I was stunned. It saddened me to look at her. Devra's hair was uncombed, and her clothes looked like she'd slept in them. The cute condo was a wreck, and it was evident that several people were living there. There was no curio. There were no trinkets. Devra talked about how much she missed Janine. I told her I missed her, too. I invited Devra to lunch. Her excuses about not being able to meet broke my heart. I thought about Janine asking me to look after Devra and felt helpless.

Almost one year after her mother died, Devra was gone. Just like that. I received a phone call and was told she'd died. No explanation. Two weeks later, I was in the same mortuary where Janine's service was held. It was time to say goodbye to Devra.

It seemed so senseless. Most of all, it seemed so avoidable. Devra isolated herself and never sought help. A family member shared how they desperately tried to help her. Still, Devra refused or made promises she would later break. She sold items to support her habit. It seems shameful to share such information about the deceased. Yet, I'm compelled to share. The sober, vibrant Devra I knew would want to help someone. She gave advice—good advice—freely but found it impossible to take advice. I hope at least one reader will find a way to reach someone in crisis.

This sad story does not have to be yours. Devra had time to prepare for her mother's death. It was not sudden; she knew when her condition became untreatable. Devra made a choice. While still sober, she avoided conversations to prepare for life without her mother. She never wanted to hear words meant to encourage her to live. Once Janine was gone, she didn't have the strength to face life without her.

If you feel the weight of depression or sadness is too heavy to find a reason to look forward to living, please remember Devra. Remember Janine's wishes for her daughter. Choose to live for your loved one and yourself. If making a choice seems out of your control, please ask for help. Seek help as if your life depends on it because it just might.

<u>Acceptance</u>

Imagine a cozy living room with plants in macramé holders hanging from the ceiling. Glass sliding doors offer a view of the pool from the sofa where my aunt sits. It is early evening after dinner, and the dishes are washed. My sister and I are playing video games and sharing candy with our cousins when I decide to walk away. I enter the living room to watch my aunt. I sit in a chair, which seems extra large for a little girl like me. I pretend to look through the window, but I'm there to watch Aunt Betty.

The brightest light in the room glows above her head as she reads. It doesn't take long for her to notice me.

"Hi, Dawn," she said. She looked pleasantly surprised.

"Hi, Aunt Betty," I immediately walked over to the couch and sat down. Her warm arm had just enough cushion to feel better than the pillows. "What's it about?"

Aunt Betty gladly told me about the bible scriptures she was reading. I wish I could remember what they were. I do remember watching her read a lot during our two-week summer visit. I'll never forget how she nibbled at her bottom lip while reading or clipping grocery coupons. Her eyes were serious when she read, but when she laughed, they outshined the stars.

My memories of Aunt Betty don't stop there. Visits and Thanksgiving weekends in her home were priceless because of her. My last visit is just as memorable, but for all the wrong reasons.

It seemed so wrong to get the news that Aunt Betty had breast cancer. It was painful for the family, yet we tried to remain hopeful. Aunt Betty left us but not without a fight. She refused surgery and turned to holistic remedies. She lived for nine years after her diagnosis. During the last year of her life, she called me a few times to search for information on the Internet about a remedy she heard about. We all have our opinions about what she should or should not have done. As for me, I'm glad she had a choice to live on her terms. She lived to see her youngest graduate and become an adult. When facing a daunting diagnosis, perhaps that's more than we can ask for.

When I arrived for my last visit to her home, I walked past the cozy living room. It looked almost the same, but the air was heavy, and so were my feet. I dragged myself down the hall. While eager to see her, I dreaded this visit.

"Hi, Aunt Betty!" I said with quiet enthusiasm. My daughter was a toddler and held onto the bottom of my shirt as I bent down to hug my aunt.

Happy to see me, two of her siblings, and her oldest daughter gathered in the room; she smiled. For a few minutes, everything seemed normal. She was sitting in bed and telling her daughter to get her pocketbook. She instructed her about some money, what she wanted from the store, and to get her checkbook for her. For the next few minutes, she chatted while balancing her bank account. That was Friday. On Saturday, more family members gathered in a circle around her to pray. After the last amen, Aunt Betty said, "I may not be winning this race, but I'm still in it." I will never forget those words. When I feel discouraged, I remember her words and find the strength to encourage myself as she did.

By Sunday morning, her health had declined. She was no longer able to turn her head or open her eyes, but she could hear and speak. She weakly squeezed my hand as I held hers.

"I love you, Aunt Betty," I said as I planted many kisses on her face.
"I love you, too, Dawn," she said with a faint voice.

I left the room and looked at my cousin. So many lines suddenly crossed her face as she strained to keep from crying about her mom. As soon as we embraced, we both welcomed the relief of crying in one another's arms.

Aunt Betty did not complain as she continued her *race*. She is a beautiful example of a person who understands acceptance. She did not want the process of dying to keep her from living, no matter how much time she had left. I encourage survivors to do the same as they grieve. As difficult as it may be, find acceptance, and be determined to focus on living.

Survivor's Nuggets

Getting closer to acceptance might tempt you to celebrate the completion of the process. Days or weeks later, you may feel like you're right back to anger or any other stage of grief. It is perfectly normal. Acknowledge what is happening and try to determine what may have triggered it. As stated earlier, you will never *get over* significant losses. You don't get over it; you get through it.

In the process of getting through it, you will start planning how to live without the person. You choose to make new connections and create new norms. You find yourself having more good days than bad days. You realize paying attention to your needs does not mean you're denying your feelings or betraying your loved one.

Finding Value

When Elisabeth Kübler-Ross wrote *On Death and Dying* in 1969, she introduced the Five Stages of Grief to the world. The book focused on what the dying have to teach others. She established fundamental definitions of each stage, which set the foundation for more work and books to be written about the subject. David Kessler later joined Kübler-Ross as co-author of *On Grief and Grieving* to explain how the process of grief teaches us to live with loss.

While writing *Survivor's Nuggets*, I was pleased to learn that Kessler released a book in 2019 entitled *Finding Meaning: The Sixth Stage of Grief*. This stage truly resonates with me because I've always believed in finding value in spite of loss; in looking for the cloud's silver lining. What we learn from an awful experience and our ability never to give up hope are, for me, necessary values. I'm no Pollyanna, but I do believe life is to be appreciated and valued.

The more you love someone, the more you hurt when you lose them, even if they lived a long and happy life as my first-grade teacher did. I felt such guilt when she died until I found the words she wrote to me...

I walked into the first-grade classroom and immediately inhaled fragrances I would remember for decades: the smell of chalk on the blackboard; a pleasantly odd scent I later learned was ink from the mimeograph machine; and a lovely perfume floating toward me from a woman with the softest, sweetest eyes that twinkled when she smiled.

"Good morning! Come in, children. Find a seat. We must begin," Mrs. Posnack said with as much excitement as I had fluttering around in my stomach. This was a huge day. The most important of my life thus far. My parents decided to keep me home during what would have been my kindergarten year. They wanted me to stay home with my sister so we could start school the same year—so no kindergarten for me. My mother played school with us; we had our very own blackboard at home. My mother and father often read to us at bedtime. My sister and I had each other to socialize with. I never felt I missed anything by not going to kindergarten.

My mother and I met the principal and toured the school a few days prior, and I was ready. So ready! I had my very own book bag with supplies, new clothes, and shiny new shoes.

I sat up straight in my chair with my hands folded on my desk. I didn't know what to expect; the only teacher I'd ever known was *Mommy*. Mrs. Posnack had an authoritative yet kind voice. She made her expectations known. Each day, we learned a little more about the routines we would follow for the next nine months. I. Loved. Every. Minute. I already knew how to read lots of words, tell time, write, count, and add. My mom did a great job, right?! I loved watching her and my father read to us;

it made me act like an adult as I read to my little sister. I often pretended to be her teacher. And here I was in a real school! I sat at my little wooden desk and drank in every new skill Mrs. Posnack taught us. She often called on me to read aloud and help others after I completed my work. I felt special. She made me feel special.

When first grade came to an end in June, I had mixed feelings about leaving. I didn't know how to express how excited I was to go to second grade because I was too sad to leave Mrs. Posnack. In her unique way, Mrs. Posnack seemed to know just how I felt. She created a special hall pass that read, "Mrs. Posnack, Room 202." She explained that whenever I completed my work, I could ask my second-grade teacher to allow me to help the new first graders in her classroom. What a perfect arrangement; I could grow up and move on without leaving my beloved Mrs. Posnack. I saw her each day until sixth-grade graduation. Once I started junior high school, Mrs. Posnack and I exchanged letters twice a month. When I later married and moved across the country, the letters continued, and there were occasional phone calls. I visited her a few times as well. One particular visit included a special treat. I got to see her Brooklyn apartment: pictures of her family, all the trinkets that made the place hers. I saw mementos of her husband and her treasured piano. She played a tune and sang—oh my goodness—it was the bunny song! Mrs. Posnack had written a song about a bunny and would sing it for us in the class while playing her piano. I was taken right back to Room 202. I listened to her voice and the music; I could smell the chalk and her perfume all over again.

Survivor's Nuggets

Thirty-six years after I entered that room as a first-grader, I called Mrs. Posnack and heard a tone that struck my chest, followed by the words *no longer in service*. I made myself inhale deeply and searched for her son's number. He explained that his mother had died a few weeks before; it was four months before my next promised visit. She was 92 years old, and I should have been happy that she enjoyed a long life, loved her husband, and enjoyed her teaching career. She enjoyed trips to Maine every summer—I received postcards—and she cherished being a mother and grandmother. Those thoughts would come later. At that moment, I was struck with sadness and guilt. Why didn't I go sooner than I'd planned? She said she would wait for me, and I took it more lightly than I should have because she often spoke of getting old and how much the world had disappointingly changed.

The letters! I had boxes of letters and cards with sweet messages from Mrs. Posnack. I pulled one box out and read for a long time. The guilt subsided a bit. She wrote about romance and love being so much more important than money. She wrote about her summers in Maine, replenishing her for each new school year. She eventually wrote about getting old and told me to delay it as long as possible. Her last letters often asked forgiveness: she knew her handwriting had become more difficult to read, so she apologized for that. She even wrote, "I'm sorry for being such a drag. Getting old is not all it's cracked up to be." Letters like those prompted me to call her. She always sounded so excited to hear me on the other end. She knew I loved her, and she loved me.

It's been years since her death, and I still shed a tear if I think too long about certain words she shared, her hug, her perfume, and, most of all, her voice and smile. I've learned to welcome those moments and be grateful for the lasting impact Mrs. Posnack has on my heart. The guilt I felt about not going to see her sooner did not simply vanish into thin air. It slowly decreased with time because I was able to reflect on so many good memories. And I forgave myself. More importantly, I learned to find value in grief. Yes, value! No one wants to lose a loved one. No one welcomes suffering, but each of us has or will experience grief and loss. When we allow ourselves to experience the grief stages, we should reach the stage of acceptance and, ultimately, the stage I call *Finding Hope and Value*.

Scripture says we should find joy in all things. Attempting to do so while grieving may sound ludicrous, but it isn't impossible. There is joy in finding hope and value in the lessons learned during the most challenging life experiences. These are the valuable nuggets we can use to encourage ourselves and to enlighten others.

I honestly believe that most experiences in life have purpose—even the most difficult. Mrs. Posnack represented hope in a lot of ways. As I continued to grow and mature, she was still my teacher. She was one who created so much wonder when she taught. She told me on numerous occasions that I should become a teacher. I should have realized that was confirmation because my mother told me the same for years! I scoffed at the idea and thought I had it all figured out. After a career that involved writing contracts and assisting minority business owners, I became a licensed real estate agent. That was fun for a while until the time between commission checks seemed to be a bit too long. I started teaching as a substitute for extra funds and fell in love with it. I went back to school and earned my first Master's degree, and acquired a teaching license. My mother was thrilled, and we continue to have wonderful talks about education.

I became a teacher after Mrs. Posnack's death. She never knew after all those years of urging me to teach that I'd become a teacher. Feeling regretful compelled me to call her son to let him know. I smiled as I held the telephone to my ear. I told him about becoming a teacher and that I wanted him to know since I couldn't tell Mrs. Posnack. He was appreciative and said that teaching is such a noble profession, and his mother would be proud. Talking to him was the next best thing to calling her.

Extra Nuggets

Laughter

Laughter. The very word makes us think of happy times, parties, favorite music, and inside jokes. Some laugh when nervous, and it is usually apparent that they don't believe the situation is funny. I learned how valuable laughter could be in the face of loss. Initially, laughter seems out of place. I know someone whose laughter got on my nerves until I experienced the relief it brought at the darkest of times.

My dear friend Della would laugh at the oddest times: her cancer scare, the day she and her husband threw the Christmas tree at each other, and unemployment. Her laughter at the *wrong* time bothered me for years. One day that all changed. I was going through a particularly ugly divorce that put me in a tailspin of emotions. My friend sat in her kitchen 2,527 miles away and made me laugh about my pending court date and all the trimmings that would go with it.

"Hey, don't be nervous. You need us to come out there?" Della asked while giggling. I was quiet, and she didn't wait for an answer.

"I'll bring the whole family—they don't know about Brooklyn. We don't play!" She let out a louder giggle, and I cracked up. I still remind Della of how she helped me appreciate laughter. Years later, I still believe laughter helps soothe physical and emotional pain. By the way, she and her husband both laugh about that Christmas tree as they continue to enjoy decades of marriage.

Thoughts of Della's laughter were welcomed when years later, on a July afternoon, I entered Jean's hospice room. As a hospice volunteer, I visited so many just like it over the years. The room was quiet and softly lit. Some might call it lonely and sad; others might embrace the peace and stillness it had. Unlike hopeful expectations for some hospital patients, here, each outcome is predictable. We know what to expect from hospice. We're typically not expecting a cure, healing, or patient to return to her home. The typical hospice patient and their family are preparing for the final days. I visit the patient hoping she and her family and friends have accepted that death is imminent. I hope they trust the hospice staff and volunteers to do all we can to ensure the patient will rarely be in pain or alone; servitude—caring for others selflessly—the Creator's work.

Cards were placed in each room to alert visitors to particular circumstances or instructions. Jean's card stated that she'd lost her vision, would talk during visits, and slept often. Volunteers are never given the patient's diagnosis. Quite frankly, we don't need it.

Jean immediately asked, "What's it like outside?" As I swept my hair up with a clip to let my neck cool, I said, "It's so hot," and immediately added, "But it's a very lovely day. It's bright and sunny, and the breeze is blowing the leaves right outside your window." She seemed to like that and smiled softly. Relieved that I hadn't continued to complain about the weather, which Jean could not feel or see, I walked closer to her bedside. To my surprise, Jean said something about being cold, so I asked if she'd like me to pull her blanket over her shoulders. "No, no, not yet," she said giggling. After silently moving her lips a few times, she found her voice and said, "I'll be really *cold* later." She let another giggle escape, a bit louder this time. I thought of Della's laughter.

"But I'm ready. I'm ready to go...to go, uh," she paused for several seconds.

I quietly said, "My uncle called it an adventure." Memories of being with my uncle two weeks before he died flooded my thoughts for a second.

"Yes!" she said as if an exclamation point had suddenly dropped from the sky. "That's good. An adventure." She giggled again, and I, too, knew it was good.

I'm thankful for my little visit. I hope Jean's enjoying her adventure.

Ralph Waldo Emerson said, "Laugh in the face of adversity"—easier said than done—and people like Della and Jean continue to prove it's possible to do. My mother recently realized that she often says something funny during sad times. She believes this is her way of combating overwhelming sadness, even if the relief is momentary. In a Psychology Today article, Dr. Marilyn Mendoza wrote the following:

> *"A study done at Kent State and reported in the American Journal of Hospice and Palliative Care revealed that humor was present in 85 percent of 132 observed nurse-based visits. Amazingly, they found that 70 percent of the humor was initiated by the patient. If humor is a part of living, then why should it not be a part of dying?... One of the tasks of grieving is to learn to laugh again."* ("The Healing Power of Laughter in Death and Grief," Psychology Today, n.d.)

Dr. Mendoza is focusing on an area we should probably explore more deeply–for ourselves as well as for those we love. It is expected and accepted that grief, death, and dying are sad. I feel compelled to let people know it's okay to laugh again. A dying person who uses humor to cope and manage feelings should be encouraged to do so. The old cliché, *laughter is good medicine*, is not so cliché after all. It's an extra nugget, a hidden treasure discovered at the most unexpected time.

Assurance

Assurance is something we often discover after a loved one has died. Assurance is what we search for when we have questions, doubts, worries, and unresolved guilt or anger about our loved one. I discovered the gift of assurance through the process of grief. The remaining stories explain how.

On April 23, 2005, Uncle Bruddy went on an adventure. Three weeks before that cloudy, dreary day, he was propped up in the hospital bed in the basement of his home. Uncle Bruddy's house was once a lively venue for get-togethers, card games, and dances with the family. Sitting in his lovely home in North Bellmore, Long Island, the only lively thing appeared to be the big screen TV, until I looked into my uncle's eyes. His cheeks were sunken, and his body was like a feather, a look so common among cancer patients. But his eyes were still alive, and in them, I could still see the uncle who would pull my two braids and say, "Ding dong, Avon calling," throughout my childhood. The corniest memories are also the sweetest. I can still hear him imitate Donald Duck with a voice that made me feel I was magically sent to Disney World.

Uncle Bruddy was one of the stars of my mother's childhood and life. He was her *Gooeyslosh* (the nickname they called each other after he returned from overseas—he was so handsome in his Air Force uniform!). He was her big brother, and she adored him. My mother admits she was the reason for a lot of laughing and teasing as a girl. She recently shared that she did or said silly things—announcing she would one day name her daughter Spatula—just for a laugh. Several relatives thought she was serious; for my mother, that made her antics even funnier. Gooeyslosh laughed with her, not at her, and had the ability to make her feel extra special. Mommy thought Uncle

Bruddy called the Air Force food *gooey slosh*, but that wasn't the case. To this day, we have no idea where the odd nickname came from!

My thoughts often take me back to that basement. Uncle Bruddy wasn't having such a good day, so my mother and I stayed for a short time and went back the next day. This time he was a little stronger and was out of bed. In his chair, he sat on a special pillow their eldest sister bought for him to ease the discomfort. His wife had just gone upstairs with a laundry basket, leaving us alone with my uncle. I wondered if she was trying to keep life as normal as possible, no matter how impossible.

I was on a mission. I had my bible—the small one I keep in my purse or car when traveling—and communion containers, each filled with grape juice and a wafer. Uncle Bruddy's feet were elevated, and we sat in chairs facing him. Mommy placed his feet in her lap and gently massaged them. She has a quiet way of doing something sweet. I love that.

"Now Dawndy," Uncle Bruddy always used my childhood nickname, "Are you licensed to do this?" His smiling eyes still had that twinkle I saw a million times as a child. I was a little surprised by his question.

"To share communion? No, I don't need a license for that. Communion is our way of remembering what Jesus did for us."

I started to turn to 1 Corinthians 11:23–26 but looked up at him, "Uncle Bruddy, do you believe in God?" My heart was thumping in my ears.

"Sure," he said as he lifted his arms and looked up, "I mean, look at this world." My heartbeat was normal again.

"Gooeyslosh, that's messing up your pants there." His skin was flaking onto my mother's lap as she massaged his feet.

"You know that's dead skin." She later told me that she cringed at the word *dead*, but answered, "No, no, it's okay," not caring one bit, and kept rubbing his feet. He insisted she place a paper towel under his feet, so she did.

I proceeded to read from First Corinthians when mid-sentence, my uncle recited, from memory, the entire passage I'd outlined with my yellow highlighter. I closed my mouth and widened my eyes. When he finished, he looked at me and said, "You didn't think I knew that, huh?" His face had a look of mischief usually found on the face of a child. Before I could answer, he asked, "Do you believe in the resurrection?"

"Absolutely. Do you?"

"Sure. Well, okay," as he waved toward the communion containers. After giving one to each of them, I picked up my own and prayed the sinner's prayer and read the communion verses in First Corinthians. A communion wafer and juice never tasted so good.

I collected the empty containers, and Uncle Bruddy broke out in a song. It was a hymn unknown to me, but the words described the cross and the resurrection. My mother and I were overwhelmed.

Weeks before my visit, Uncle Bruddy tried to ease my mother's attempt to accept what was happening to him. Perhaps he felt as if he were back in Brooklyn teaching his little sister to pronounce Schenectady Avenue. "Now, Gooeyslosh, it's okay. I'm going on an adventure," he explained to her. These are the words that comfort her today. He was unique, and we each enjoyed the journey of his life. The last leg of his journey, he had to take without us. Uncle Bruddy made it clear that he looked forward to his adventure.

On the first anniversary of his death, my mother was in New York, and I called her. "It's another cloudy, dreary day just like it was last year," she said in a voice that welcomed the clouds. In some way, even the clouds were acknowledging her Gooeyslosh.

I said, "Yeah, it's nice to think that you can cry along with the rain. You know how everything is so clean and new after it rains?" I could hear her smiling over the phone.

More than a decade later, my mother continues to be comforted by the nugget of assurance Gooeyslosh left her:

his explanation of his adventure. He once pointed at the sky and said, "See there? Well, way beyond there. That's where I'm going on an adventure. And it's okay." His voice was very matter-of-fact, positive, and sure. And there was peace in that then, and peace and assurance now.

For those who are unsure or even fearful of the inevitable end of life, I hope knowing there can be an adventure awaiting each of us brings a modicum of peace. In this life, most of us are willing to share good news and fortune. How much more compelled are we to share when we have what we believe is an absolute assurance of life after death? We are committed to wanting the same assurance for others, especially our loved ones. Think about my Uncle Bruddy; he was not a church member as an adult. I never saw him read a bible and never heard him speak of salvation. What he did do was live his life as an example. He was not perfect; he was uniquely flawed like any other human being. But he did not forget the scriptures he was taught as a child. Knowing that my uncle was sure of his next *adventure* helped us to say good-bye because we actually meant *so long for now*. When you reflect on your life as you age and ponder what may become of you, I hope you will remember this story. I hope you will consider the ultimate hope and assurance.

The promise and peace associated with assurance—I like to refer to it as *blessed assurance*—resonate with me when I think of several people I've said good-bye to. One, in particular, is Clifford.

I pictured him in heaven. I absolutely believed he was there and wondered how it was. Despite believing that heaven exists and attending countless funerals over the years, this was the first time I continuously thought about someone being there. Sure, I think others found their eternal rest there, but I often found my thoughts straying to what being there must be like for Clifford. I was experiencing a new way of reflecting after losing a loved one.

Knowing that he believed in God would later be a source of consolation. At the time, my husband and I were just sad. Clifford was too young. He had a daughter who depended on him, and he was a good person. Such a simple word, *good*, and that he was in so many ways. Clifford was a natural servant. He put others before himself, sometimes to a fault. He was eager to make sure he did whatever he could to help his parents, aunts, and uncles. Rarely did a smile leave his warm face. He was my husband's cousin who lovingly called me *Cuz*. I miss him.

I'll never forget one particular day. My husband and I offered to help Clifford to clean and organize his parents' home. A few other relatives joined us and worked on separate areas of the house. Clifford and I spent most of the day together. He played his favorite gospel songs on a CD player and sang along as we worked. He stopped throughout the day to show me a photo or trinket on a shelf and explained why each held sentimental value. His eyes could no longer hold back tears as he explained, "Cuz, I feel like I'm cleaning up because my parents are no longer here, but they are. I can't imagine what it'll feel like when they're really gone." He was sharing what many people think about losing parents. These are natural thoughts; we believe the expected order of life is that we will survive them. Clifford never experienced such loss. He died. His mother and father were left with the unspeakable task of burying their son.

Just like that, he was gone. We knew of some health issues, but his exit was unexpected and piercing. The CD he played that day in his parents' home is still one of our favorites. You see, months before his death, Clifford sent copies of that CD to several relatives, and what a gift it was. As we drove home after Clifford's funeral, we listened to the CD. We were quiet. My husband and I squeezed each other's hands. As we pulled into the garage, he said, "I want to sit here and listen to this first."

"Me too," I whispered. The lyrics of *He Favored Me* filled the air, and we both wept. It was so incredibly sad.

What are we to learn from this profoundly sad and untimely death? Maybe being an educator or someone who seeks the cloud's silver lining made me ponder what we are to learn from such a tragic loss. On so many levels, some death experiences are seemingly meaningless. I think it's because we're focusing on death and not life. Without discounting the importance of sharing our feelings, perhaps we should shift our focus when looking for meaning. Sometimes there is no meaning. I believe some deaths are senseless. A child killed by a drunk driver has no meaning in this context. Such senseless deaths have, however, spawned positive action for change.

When possible, I believe we should focus on how a person lived, what they contributed, and how they impacted others. Clifford was a servant at heart. He passed through this life as an example of what we all should be to one another—servants. How can we improve the life or experience of a relative, neighbor, friend, or even a stranger? Tangible gifts are easy answers. What about the intangible? What can a smile, a hug, or a visit do for a fellow human being? *Do unto others* is at the heart of being a dedicated servant. Knowing Clifford was precisely that allows us to honor him. As time passed, the sting of saying good-bye hurt a little less. It was comforting to think of him being in heaven.

Guilt and Gratitude

Guilt is a heavy load to carry. When we feel guilty, we often feel ashamed; I know I do. It interferes with our ability to be productive and makes it difficult to process the various stages of grief. Guilt was so heavy for me that I tried to ignore it while writing this book. Remember the story about Mrs. Posnack? Initially, I tried writing her story without bringing up my feelings of guilt because it made me so sad and a little embarrassed. I think guilt is often linked to embarrassment. I told Mrs. Posnack I would see her during my visit to New York in August. "I'll try to wait for you to get here, my darling." I took her words for granted—she died in April—the August visit never happened.

Perhaps losing Mrs. Posnack led me to make two trips to New York in a matter of weeks when my uncle's health had become worse. Guilt made me question why I had not simply made other arrangements to visit during spring break. That's where the bargaining came in. If I only did this or did that. Well, then what? Perhaps one more visit, and we could have had some closure. But would we? Did we miss the chance to have a final conversation? Were we supposed to wrap up the decades of teaching, learning, letters, phone calls, and memories? Maybe. It took some time to convince myself that she knew how much I loved her. I know she loved me even though I didn't make it there in time.

Imagine the horror I felt when I made another phone call one year and six months later to learn about yet another passing. Guilt reared its ugly head again, and I told myself I deserved it.

Angela Pernatozzi was the life of Classroom On Wheels (C.O.W.)—the ball of energy that kept C.O.W.'s inner workings alive and growing. Before meeting Angela, I heard the organization's founder speak with such passion that it broke my heart. She stood in the center of the room during a United Way training designed to recruit more people of color to serve on nonprofit organizations' boards. Her attractive face suddenly tightened, and her cheeks were flushed as tears pooled in her eyes. She told a story—of a five-year-old who inspired her to become the Las Vegas mobile preschool classroom founder—that she would repeat again and again. I saw beyond her teary eyes and shaky but determined voice, "How can we turn our heads when a 5-year-old asks, 'which one is the red crayon?' and pretend that's okay?" I committed to joining the C.O.W. board of directors that day.

At the time, kindergarten was not mandatory in the state of Nevada. The lower-income communities suffered the most. Without mandatory kindergarten, many students entered first-grade classrooms with little or no preparation. Enter the C.O.W. bus! An old school bus was donated and painted white with black cow spots. The interior of the bus was gutted. Without seats, there was plenty of room to create a preschool classroom. The community rallied around C.O.W. Generous donations allowed the organization to acquire a fleet of C.O.W.s to travel into neighborhoods and educate children. I could not wait to contribute as a board member.

It was such a privilege and a pleasure to work with Angela. She was the Executive Director of Classroom On Wheels. She was small in stature, but there was nothing small about her smile, heart, and passion for children. She would later share stories of entertaining the residents of Ohio Valley as Kabbie the Clown. She had such funny and colorful stories that made her eyes light up with each word.

I loved visiting with her and enjoyed our telephone calls. One day my phone rang, and after saying hello, I heard, "Pernatozzi here. Think ya could get this computer to work?" Hearing her hearty chuckle made me smile. Angela's exaggerated accent had a way of cracking me up. I could never tell if she wanted to sound like a New Yorker or a girl from Philly! I looked forward to seeing her during one of many lunch hours to help with the computers. Her office was only a few minutes away from mine, and she often called me to assist her or a staff member. I gladly obliged.

Angela was exceptionally talented. She was interviewed by countless media members, wrote grants, attended many graduation ceremonies of the C.O.W. students, and was instrumental in establishing two more *COWs*: Clinic On Wheels and Computers on Wheels. In her typical humble way, she praised others, but it was her unique personality that gave C.O.W. life. She had countless jokes to really *moooove* a person to laughter. Cow figurines, posters, and magnets were tastefully placed all over her office. Angela put the *moo* in every word she could!

As funny as she was, she was also very tender. When I shared that I'd become a mom through the wonder of adoption, she was so happy for me. She was tickled to learn that she and my daughter shared the same birth date. She was kind and honest when I wrestled with the battle of divorce, and later when I started to date again. We enjoyed a ladies' tea at a local mansion, which was almost as lovely as she was. I will never forget that day and the years of memories.

I lost touch with Angela. That's what we say when we no longer call or visit people, right? I called her home for a *long time, no see* chat. Her husband answered the phone and was silent when I asked for her. He gently told me that she died. That sinking feeling I've had while holding the phone and listening to unbearable news flushed my body again. Heat ripped through my stomach, and I felt my heartbeat in my throat.

I had to accept that I'd never be able to call or see her again. It was a moment to reflect and thank God for her. I could not possibly forgive myself at that moment, but I forced myself to be thankful. Remembering someone so colorful, excited about life, and ready to laugh would later comfort me. Why didn't I keep in touch? I didn't even know she had cancer. Had it been that long since we talked? I could have comforted her. We could have had more time together if I had only kept in touch. I kicked myself and cried. This bargaining stage was intertwined with guilt. Not calling Angela sooner was a grave reminder to make relationships a priority, no matter what. I wasn't suffering from an illness or anything that would keep me from nurturing our friendship. At that time, the company I was working for downsized. After 14 years of service, my position was eliminated. Divorced and out of a job, I started a new career. I showed my young daughter a happy face even when I didn't feel so happy. I allowed the whirlwind of changes in my life to distract me from keeping in touch.

So here I was again, repeating the same promises to myself that I made a year and a half earlier when Mrs. Posnack died. When I caught myself saying, "Okay, next time..." I stopped and held my breath. I thought how ridiculous my attempt to plan for *next time* sounded. No, it was time to do something new. I sat down and wrote about Angela. I found her obituary and picture online and read an article about her as well. I felt happy for her. Wishing she had won the battle and lived will never go away. But I found peace in knowing that she did so many things with the time she had. I admired her example of being selfless. She was passionate about working and volunteering for worthy causes. I forgave myself. I do my best to keep in touch more often with those I love. I am forever grateful for the time Angela and I did have together. I replaced guilt with gratitude.

As a hospice volunteer, I co-facilitated a grief support group. The experience allowed me to guide children, teenagers, and adults through their grief journey. One day, an attendee said, "I just can't wait to be over this. I'm tired of living like this and crying all the time." I asked her to describe what being *over this* meant. Her answers were predictable: not feeling sad anymore, the crying would stop, eating more regularly, and enjoying a good night's sleep. These are perfectly reasonable expectations. I asked what made her cry. She said pictures, songs, special days like her father's birthday, and holidays. I carefully explained that she would probably feel sad when those days come around each year for the rest of her life, but it would sting a little less as time went on. We ended the session by engaging the group members in an exercise to celebrate their loved ones. Each person had experienced the loss of a loved one within the past year. Therefore, the pain was fresh for each of them. Acceptance was not a stage they had the joy of experiencing yet.

The other co-facilitators and I explained that each of them would be given a large feather. Each feather had a green plastic leaf attached to it. They were asked to write a final message to their loved one on the leaf. Often, when we lose a loved one, we have feelings of guilt or remorse about not telling them something we may have held onto for years. This exercise was their chance to express those feelings.

Once all the group members had written on their leaves, we escorted them to one of the outdoor areas of the hospice campus. We stopped in front of a tall, mature tree where the leaves would be placed. It was completely silent as each person tied their leaf to a tree branch. Afterward, a few shared what they'd written, but no one was forced to do so. A few clapped, others hugged, there were a few tears, and many smiled.

Doing this allowed the attendees to express themselves. Some released words that kept them stuck in a particular stage of grief. Others felt the exercise provided a sense of closure. I hope and pray that they continue to feel relieved and allow themselves to embrace acceptance eventually. It is often easier to let go of the stages of grief that bind us when we make an outward gesture like hanging the leaves on the tree. Of course, the deceased could not read the messages. This exercise was for the survivors—people who needed to share a message with someone no longer here, found comfort in writing their messages.

Forgiveness

Asking for forgiveness is often difficult to do. If you desire forgiveness from the deceased, you may feel incredibly hopeless. I walked my friend Rita through her journey to find forgiveness and hope.

I met Rita five years after her mother died. She was always very pleasant and upbeat. The closer we became, the more I realized how deeply she still hurt about her mother's death. I have yet to lose either of my parents. I can only imagine the immense pain and grief I will experience. Rita often spoke of things she wished she would have told her mother. One afternoon, the pain was so hard Rita could barely speak. She wept for what seemed like two hours. She talked as she sobbed. Her words were hard to understand, but I just let her go.

When she pulled herself together, I suggested she write a letter to her mother. I knew she needed to take action to rid herself of that sense of helplessness. She stared at me and didn't say a word. I told her to write a letter about all the things she wanted her mother to know. I suggested she take the letter to the gravesite, read it to her mother, and then destroy it. I explained that destroying the letter would be an outward expression of releasing feelings that weighed her down.

    Like so many people, Rita had never really grieved. She cried when she looked at her mother's pictures. She spoke of her mom often and wished she were still here. She prayed. In her own words, Rita told me she really didn't grieve because she was too busy. She was responsible for the arrangements, lots of other paperwork, and caring for her mother's estate. She went to the funeral but did not join her family at the cemetery and repass. And there we were five years later. A whole five years and Rita was finally ready to take control of the process of grieving. She was preparing herself to accept her mother's death so that she could fully live. Rita acknowledged feelings of guilt and regret. I explained how these feelings could easily weaken a person, make them less confident, and unsure of what to do next.

    Rita agreed that it was important to write the words she wished she'd told her mother before she died. She also knew it was important to ask her mother to forgive her. What she didn't realize was the need to forgive herself. Rita wrote the letter and read it at her mother's gravesite. She then destroyed the letter and was determined to get stronger. Rita chose to accept that she could not change the order of events. There was nothing she could do about unspoken words with her mother. Rita chose to honor her mother and continue to live in ways that would make her proud.

Once the burden of carrying unresolved feelings—expressed in the letter—Rita was free to accept forgiveness and live.

Writing may also provide you with the release that Rita experienced. Write about what you feel and why. Help yourself to discover the reasons for your feelings. Then determine if you need to forgive others, ask for forgiveness, or forgive yourself. Do all of the above without guilt or shame. You are human, and you're acknowledging your pain. Reward yourself for recognizing the need for forgiveness. Remember that you're also releasing emotions you no longer need to own.

The Journal and The Bio

References to my journal are consistent threads throughout the fabric of this book. Writing in a journal about life experiences has been priceless for me. With each journal entry, I reflected on an experience, processed how I felt, and concluded with what I learned. Writing in a journal has been most helpful for me when writing about two things: my dreams and loss. All the stories about the latter are the basis of this book.

I encourage you to write. If your preference is to speak, use a speech-to-text feature on your computer, tablet, or phone. Either way, you will have a documented history of your reflections and ideas.

Survivor's Nuggets

Because I feel so strongly about regularly writing in a journal, I prepared a guideline for you. The following pages have two sections: 'Survivor's Nuggets: The Journal' and 'Survivor's Nuggets: Write Your Life Story.' In the first section, I explain the benefits of writing in a journal while processing grief. In the second section, I provide instructions to guide you through writing your life story. I hope you take advantage of both.

Survivor's Nuggets: The Journal

Has anyone ever told you that journaling is cathartic, therapeutic, or relaxing? Perhaps you read about similar advice. Others may suggest writing about something you're grateful for. When you're grieving after a significant loss, it may not be easy to get started. Have you received a beautiful journal and promised yourself to start writing? Are the pages still empty? Or have you started writing, only to suddenly find yourself stuck? All answers are perfectly normal and part of the process. The fact that you have or are willing to consider writing in a journal is a promising way to begin.

Let's dive a little deeper into this discussion about journaling. How do you write when loss floods your mind? Where do you begin when you're feeling anger, guilt, sadness, loneliness, loss of control, or hopelessness? Writing about your feelings may initially seem to intensify unwanted emotions. I think that's a great start. It is an excellent way to address surface issues in order to express deep pain. I believe you can find hope after working through the pain.

You don't have to write a book. You don't have to be a fantastic writer with excellent spelling and perfect grammar. None of that matters. When writing in a journal, you are doing more than just writing. You're releasing. Holding on to all the feelings associated with your grief can be so unhealthy—mentally and physically.

I started keeping two journals years ago: one about dreams and another about visiting the terminally ill and those who lost loved ones. The latter became the foundation of this book. During each visit, someone would share words I knew I had to write about, words I would never forget. I witnessed facial expressions and gestures so sweet that I had to write about them. I watched one woman softly pat her deceased husband's face as he lay in their bedroom. I listened as a man asked parents not to push their children so hard as he spoke at his son's funeral. His son committed suicide at the age of 18. I wrote about these stories and more. The sooner I wrote, the more detailed my journal entries were.

I keep a journal on my nightstand. I often wake up in the middle of the night with an idea or a dream. A few times, I rolled over to return to sleep after promising myself to write it all down in the morning. Unable to remember all the details the next day, I decided my ideas and dreams were worth more than sleep. Now I grab my journal and write immediately after waking up. You'll find what works best for you. One suggestion is to start writing or recording your spoken words so you can revisit them later.

Journaling is a way of releasing your anger, guilt, regret, or sadness, allowing room for new emotions, new experiences, new relationships, and the proverbial *new normal*. It may be just the thing you need to get closer to reconstructing your life and accepting the loss. There is no time table. You don't wake up one day suddenly ready for your new way of life after loss. No one has the right to tell you when it's time to move forward. However, I encourage you to listen to those you trust who may worry that you're *stuck*. It is a process, sometimes a longer process than you may wish, but I believe you'll be pleased with the outcome.

Whether it is a book, an essay, or a report, I always start with an outline when I begin to write. The outline may be revised as I proceed, but it's still a great place to start. You can do the same with a journal.

Following is a sample outline to help you to take some control of your grief journey. You suffered a loss. Honor your loved one with the life you have left to live. You're a survivor. Survivors typically fight to move on. Consider using this to help you to move along your journey.

Survivor's Nuggets: The Journal Outline

A.   Description of Who You Lost

This section is similar to an introduction to your story. Write with lots of descriptive details. In fact, write this section so that a stranger reading it could picture who you lost. Describing the loss helps to move out of the stage of denial or shock.

B. How the Loss Happened

Only write the facts in this section. One way to make sure you keep it objective—no opinion or feelings—is to write this section in the style of a newspaper article. For example, if a person died in the hospital after a long battle with cancer, state that. Avoid writing how difficult it was or how sad you felt. Writing this section may help you to move away from denial.

C. How You Felt When They Died & How You Feel Now

There are no wrong ways to fill the pages of this section. Describe how you felt when your relative or friend died. Where were you when you received the news? How did you respond, and what were you feeling? Go back and read this section throughout the weeks and months after the loss. Compare how you felt when it happened with how you feel now. Your journal contains a written summary of your personal experience. Although written by you alone, you do not have to suffer in silence. If your emotions take you to a place where you feel stuck, allow yourself to call on others for help. It's your journey, but no one said you had to be alone for the entire experience.

D. Stages of Grief You Experienced

With time, your feelings will evolve because you will enter various stages in the process. You may find yourself moving toward acceptance. It is also possible to find yourself stuck in one of the stages of grief. If you discover that you are not progressing, be gentle with yourself. Analyze the words you've written in your journal. Try to determine why you're having a tough time with the stage you're in. I suggest you review the stages of grief (denial/shock, bargaining, anger, depression, acceptance) written earlier in this book. Identify the stages you experienced and describe them. Allow yourself to feel each one without apology. If you feel angry, be angry, but write about it. Writing can be your way of no longer holding on to anger or any other emotion that may disrupt your peace.

E. What You Learned (*Your Survivor's Nuggets*)

Working through the stages of grief may allow you to discover how resilient you are. What you learn about yourself is more precious than gold: your nuggets. One nugget may be realizing strength you never knew you had. Another nugget could be newfound gratitude. Write about what you've learned and the nuggets you discovered.

Survivor's Nuggets: Write Your Life Story

The most memorable parts of a funeral or memorial service are the touching or humorous stories shared by loved ones. We relate to personalized stories that make us feel close to the person who died. With enough detail and honesty, your life story can be just as impactful.

Consider writing your life story as I share a sweet experience I had with my Aunt AJ...

She was in charge and in control, but most importantly, she was prepared. AJ prepared for each stage of her life and, ultimately, her death, down to the tiniest detail. She defied the odds of a black woman born in 1930 and raised in Harlem, New York. Her high school counselor told her to pursue domestic work because she would never work in an office. Such advice did not discourage my aunt. Her counselor's discouragement motivated her to achieve.

A smile spread across my face as she told me how she had few regrets, the love of family, retired from a career she enjoyed and excelled in, and traveled around the world. She had one request: she wanted a bio and asked me to write it. Her request struck a chord because she was given six months to live three years prior.

My immediate answer was yes. However, I couldn't shake the unspoken feeling that I was actually about to write her obituary. She knew she wouldn't be here to provide the right words later. For someone like AJ, who had to get it right on her own terms, writing a bio now was perfect. I interviewed my aunt for the project. She told me stories I often heard throughout the years of my childhood. What I enjoyed most was how the new intricate details tied the old stories together.

Although diagnosed with terminal lung cancer, AJ thrived for years. She was no longer traveling but enjoyed family, friends, and all the comforts of home. She had her affairs in order. On more than one occasion, she said she was ready *to go*.

My mother lived with AJ during her final years and was more than just her sister or companion; she was her caregiver. She cooked, cleaned, shopped, and escorted her sister to a myriad of doctors' appointments. It was getting harder to help position AJ on the bed and care for her without the hospice nurse's assistance. Weeks before her death, AJ asked her younger sister, "When am I going to die? I don't like this." That was quite a moment for my mom. My mother shared what she believed that question meant. She said her sister somehow welcomed death; she did what she was here to do and was ready to go. That gave us peace.

The process of writing my aunt AJ's bio created a mixture of emotions I allowed to simmer as I worked. With each interview, waves of nostalgia washed over me. I listened to her as she painted the details of family stories and pictured relatives no longer with us. Reminiscing has a way of igniting both joy and sorrow at the same time.

Survivor's Nuggets

For those of us who embrace nostalgia, we enjoy remembering times that made us smile and laugh, and accept the experiences of pain and tears. I admit such acceptance is a lot easier when accompanied by happy memories. Hopefully, acceptance will allow us to put unpleasant memories into perspective without allowing them to destroy us. Both joy and sorrow make us human.

I was delighted by the wonderment skipping through my thoughts as I searched the Internet for photos of the family's old neighborhood, church, and schools. I poured through family photos; they were worn by time but still held the ability to awaken vivid memories. AJ's stories and details allowed me to picture the streets of Harlem, envision my older relatives as children, and smell the aroma of Mama Lily's cooking. I held my head up with pride as she described how she used racial discrimination to fuel her determination. She did land an office job and thrived in it for decades until she retired.

I mailed a copy of the final draft to AJ, hoping she wouldn't want too many changes. I certainly didn't mind making corrections, but minimal changes would mean that she was pleased. Her satisfaction was all I needed. I still have the handwritten note she sent, which stated, "Dear Dawndy, everything is so beautiful and well written. Thanks again. Love, AJ." She died a year later.

It was an honor to write Aunt AJ's bio, and it taught me that we all should consider writing our own. In the spirit of *wanting your flowers while you can still see and smell them*, writing your bio or life story may provide multiple benefits for you and your loved ones.

Seven Benefits of Writing Your Life Story

Pre-planning a funeral, cremation, or burial has become more common in recent years. However, writing an obituary before death is not as popular. Initially, some people may frown upon the idea. What may surface are the same unpleasant feelings some experience when having to discuss life insurance. Many want to avoid that conversation. Why not break that cycle of avoidance and embrace the gift of writing your life story?

The following are some benefits of writing your life story:

1. **Discovering a sense of accomplishment**

    When you reflect and assess all you've done, you can appreciate a sense of accomplishment. Remember, accomplishments are not just grandiose events that bring fame or fortune. Some of your most significant moments are things you may have overlooked, such as what a kind friend you've been or the way you made every day routines special for your children.

2. **Becoming aware of what's left on your to-do list**

    As you write your story, you may discover things you'd still like to do. I encourage you to do them. Update your life story with details of new experiences.

Survivor's Nuggets

Your life story is a *living document* as long as you're still here. Allow it to grow with you. It will become a gift cherished by those who care about you.

3. **Finding freedom in forgiveness**

A healthy assessment of your life may promote a desire for forgiveness or closure. Instead of holding on to regrets, I encourage you to address them and forgive yourself for what you did or did not do in life. If you can resolve your regrets with action, do it. Right as many wrongs as you can.

Forgiving another person is like giving them a gift, but you benefit as well. Free yourself from the bondage of holding onto anger, grudges, or guilt. The freedom of forgiveness is in the power of letting go.

4. **Telling your own story**

You get to tell your story in your own words. Who knows your story best? You! Make sure you share your story from your perspective. There is freedom and satisfaction in telling your story. There is no need for lengthy instructions here; you know best what to share and how to share it. It is your story to tell.

5. **Sparing the burden for loved ones**

You have the power to save your family from the burden of writing your obituary. While grieving, writing an obituary can be overwhelming. Avoid leaving your loved ones with this responsibility. They may have to update the information. They may even need to have your life story formatted to include in the funeral program booklet. Most importantly, you would have done the most challenging part for them.

6. **Celebrating now**

You may choose to share your life story or bio with family and friends while you can celebrate with them. Throw a party to celebrate life. If you prefer a quieter way to celebrate, share copies with those you love and enjoy individual conversations about your story. My aunt chose the latter. She mailed her bio to individual family members and friends who talked to her about it in person or on the phone. I still read her bio from time to time. I enjoy looking at the pictures that paint the story of her life. I wrote it, but it will always be her story. She is the primary creator of her bio. She left it for us as a gift of celebration.

7. **Embracing peace**

Writing your life story means you have to review your past. Some memories may be painful; however, research shows that reminiscing can increase confidence and peace. In a 2016 New York Times article, Susan B. Garland reported that after recalling how they overcame challenges in the past, study participants were better prepared to face new challenges. In awe of what they experienced in the past, many participants shared their newfound peace. Memories that were initially painful allowed them to realize their strength and to forgive themselves. One participant considered her story a "gift to future generations." Most of the study participants were older; however, it is never too early to start documenting your memories. Embrace the peace that comes with writing about your life.

How to Write Your Life Story

Let's remove the stigma you or others may be feeling. Your life story is not necessarily an obituary. Of course, you may choose to have loved ones use it when there's a need for an obituary. But right now, you are encouraged to write your life story.

Keep in mind that you may consider writing a life story for someone else before their death. That's what I did at my aunt's request. Your loved one may appreciate this unique gift but may hesitate to ask for it. Most people would probably never think to have someone do such a thing. Consider offering to write it for them and if you do, explain your relationship to the celebrated person.

One of our dearest friends is the pastor who performed our wedding ceremony. He and his wife planned a surprise appreciation banquet for my husband a few years ago. They wanted to honor him for all he has done as a youth minister, youth parole officer, athlete, and business owner. Much of what was shared by each of us that day were words we often hear at a funeral. My husband definitely received his flowers and accolades while he could enjoy them. In his own way, our pastor provided a *memorial* in the form of a celebration with family and friends. The results were heartfelt appreciation and powerful messages. Writing a life story for someone you care about can provide similar joy and satisfaction.

Before you start writing, gather your photos, and make sure you include pictures in each section described below. Consider searching the Internet for additional photos. It is amazing what can be found online. When writing my aunt's life story, I included pictures of her high school, which had been torn down decades before my search for a photo. My aunt was so surprised and pleased. If you aren't too tech-savvy, ask someone to help you. It can be a fun project to do together.

As you begin to write, refer to the following sections. Don't hesitate to add sections as you see fit—this is your life story—tell it in your unique way.

Childhood

Describe where you grew up and who you lived with; name your siblings or state that you were an only child; name your childhood friends; and describe the childhood memories most important to you. Photographs provide a visual timeline of events. Include pictures of your childhood home or neighborhood, your schools, church, favorite fun spots—parks, zoos, etc.—as well as photos of friends and relatives. Pictures will help make stories of your childhood come alive. Use your imagination.

Teen Years and Early Adulthood

Describe high school and college experiences, your first job, dating, and your significant other. Include the dreams and goals you may have had at this stage in life.

Family and Friends

People most important to you will be touched to see their names in your life story. Describe your relationships with your spouse/partner, your children, and other relatives. Include your friends and what made each of the above relationships special to you.

Current Events

Describe what life is like for you now. Bring your readers up-to-date by describing your favorite past times, foods, TV shows, movies, and music. List hobbies and the people with whom you enjoy spending time.

Words of Wisdom

We've all learned lessons during our individual journeys in life. Experiences we regret are just as meaningful as those we are proud of. Writing your life story may trigger a myriad of emotions. Remember the process of grief discussed throughout the book. What nugget did you gain from a particular loss or regret? Write it down and share it here. Use your experiences to share words of wisdom with your readers.

This section is also a great area to share traditional words of wisdom passed down from your parents, clergy, teachers, professors, coaches, business leaders, etc. The advice we treasure the most usually forms our beliefs.

Conclusion

Decide how you want to be celebrated. Perhaps sharing your written life story during intimate conversation is your style. You may prefer a small group or to meet with family and friends one by one. Another way of sharing and celebrating your life story is during a *living funeral*. Many of us have attended a funeral and thought, "Wow, if only they could hear what's going on right now." During a living funeral, attendees celebrate a person while they are still alive. I can imagine how meaningful a living funeral would be for a hospice patient because death is imminent. For others who likely have more years ahead, the event is more of a party than a living funeral. I like to think of it as a *living celebration* or a *life story gala*. Be creative—it's your party.

In *Tuesdays With Morrie: An Old Man, a Young Man, and Life's Greatest Lesson* (Albom, 2017), author Mitch Albom explains how Morrie Schwartz attended a funeral and realized that his deceased friend did not get to hear all the beautiful things that were said about him. Morrie was dying of Lou Gehrig's disease and decided to have a funeral before his death. In the Emmy-winning movie about his life produced by Oprah Winfrey, a group of singers set the atmosphere Morrie wanted. It was a living funeral, a celebration.

If you read the book, you will learn that Morrie's desire to celebrate with his friends was so like him. He was a man who cherished life and found great pleasure in giving to others. In the afterword, Albom writes about giving and taking. He explained that so many people visited Morrie with the intent to comfort him. To the visitors' surprise, they walked away in tears. Many of them shared that Morrie asked them about their problems, and they ended up being comforted by him. When Albom asked why he didn't allow them to focus on him, Morrie explained, "Mitch, why would I take like that? Taking just makes me feel like I'm dying. Giving makes me feel like I'm living." (Albom, 2017)

    Morrie's death was inevitable and something he had no control over. He was, however, in control of how he lived. He had moments of reminiscing about dancing and other activities he could no longer enjoy. While remembering his past, Morrie might have felt depressed or angry. Ultimately, he chose to move to the final stage of acceptance because doing so allowed him to focus on living. Once he accepted his diagnosis, Morrie was able to focus on celebration. His living funeral was a gift he could appreciate with his loved ones.

    Morrie's story fuels the hope others may need when facing challenges. You and I have the power to live by his example. Your sorrow is not in vain. Use your journey through the stages of grief as a testimony for someone in need of hope. Give your time and share your life story.

Survivor's Nuggets

Dear Readers,

I hope to hear from you. Hearing from my readers would be the greatest reward for me as an author. I've been thinking about you so much! Let me know what you learned about processing grief (and what more you'd like to know). I'd also love to hear about your experiences with writing your life story.

With compassion,
Dawn

Dawn Cochrane King
Email: authordawnking@gmail.com
Website: www.thejourneylessons.com
Facebook: www.bit.ly/JourneyCommunity
Amazon Author Page: www.bit.ly/AuthorDawnKing

References

Albom, M. (2017). *Tuesdays with Morrie: An old man, a young man, and life's greatest lesson, 20th Anniversary Edition.* New York: Broadway Books.

Garland, S. (2016). Telling their life stories, older adults find peace in looking back. *New York Times.* Retrieved from https://www.nytimes.com/2016/12/09/your-money/telling-their-life-stories-older-adults-find-peace-in-looking-back.html

Kessler, D. (2019). *Finding meaning: The sixth stage of grief.* New York: Scribner.

Kübler-Ross, E. (1969). *On death and dying: What the dying have to teach doctors, nurses, clergy, and their own families.* New York: Scribner.

Kübler-Ross, E., & Kessler, D. (2004). *On grief & grieving: Finding the meaning of grief through the five stages of loss.* London: Simon & Schuster.

The Healing Power of Laughter in Death and Grief | Psychology Today. Retrieved July 18, 2018, from https://www.psychologytoday.com/us/blog/understanding-grief/201611/the-healing-power-laughter-in-death-and-grief

Winfrey, O. (2011, January). Oprah's master class: Maya Angelou.

Notes

Survivor's Nuggets

Survivor's Nuggets

Survivor's Nuggets

Survivor's Nuggets

Survivor's Nuggets

Survivor's Nuggets

Survivor's Nuggets

Survivor's Nuggets

Survivor's Nuggets

Survivor's Nuggets

Survivor's Nuggets

Survivor's Nuggets

www.ingramcontent.com/pod-product-compliance
Lightning Source LLC
Chambersburg PA
CBHW070933160426
43193CB00011B/1679